Easy Rock Instrumental Solos

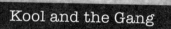

Green Day

Kool and the Gang

Evanescence

Steam

Yael Naim

Bob Seger &
The Silver Bullet Band

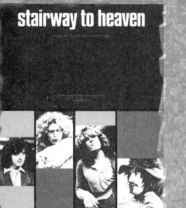

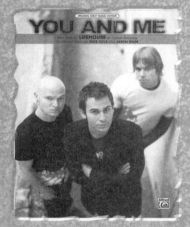

Journey

The Rolling Stones

Santana
featuring Rob Thomas

Led Zeppelin

Eagles

Lifehouse

Arranged by Bill Galliford, Ethan Neuburg and Tod Edmondson

ISBN-10: 0-7390-5987-4
ISBN-13: 978-0-7390-5987-6

CONTENTS

BOULEVARD OF BROKEN DREAMS

Words by
BILLIE JOE

Music by
GREEN DAY

4

CELEBRATION

Words and Music by
RONALD BELL, CLAYDES SMITH,
GEORGE BROWN, JAMES TAYLOR,
ROBERT MICKENS, EARL TOON,
DENNIS THOMAS, ROBERT BELL
and EUMIR DEODATO

Na Na Hey Hey Kiss Him Goodbye

Words and Music by
GARY DE CARLO, DALE FRASHUER
and PAUL LEKA

Moderate rock (♩ = 112)

Na Na Hey Hey Kiss Him Goodbye - 3 - 1
32615

10

Na Na Hey Hey Kiss Him Goodbye - 3 - 2
32615

Na Na Hey Hey Kiss Him Goodbye - 3 - 3
32615

MY IMMORTAL

Words and Music by
BEN MOODY, AMY LEE
and DAVID HODGES

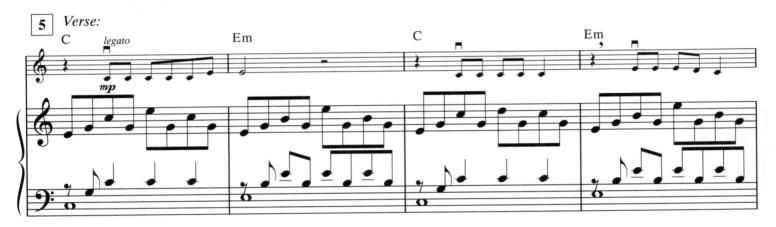

My Immortal - 4 - 1
32615

My Immortal - 4 - 2
32615

My Immortal - 4 - 4
32615

NEW SOUL

Words and Music by
YAEL NAIM and DAVID DONATIEN

Moderately (♩ = 100)

New Soul - 4 - 1
32615

SMOOTH

Words and Music by
ITAAL SHUR and ROB THOMAS

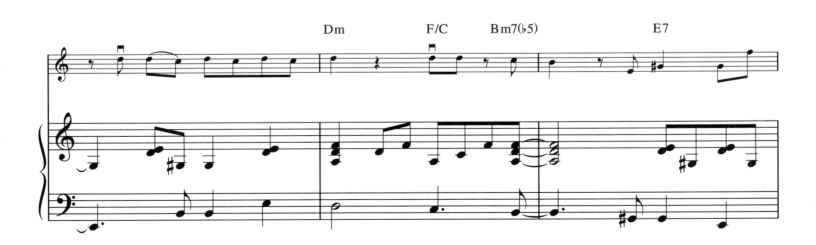

Smooth - 4 - 1
32615

OPEN ARMS

Words and Music by
JONATHAN CAIN and STEVE PERRY

Easy Rock Instrumental Solos

CONTENTS

© 2009 Alfred Publishing Co., Inc.
All Rights Reserved. Printed in USA.

ISBN-10: 0-7390-5987-4
ISBN-13: 978-0-7390-5987-6

Arranged by Bill Galliford, Ethan Neuburg and Tod Edmondson

BOULEVARD OF BROKEN DREAMS

Words by
BILLIE JOE

Music by
GREEN DAY

Moderately slow (♩ = 86)

rit.

CELEBRATION

3

Words and Music by
RONALD BELL, CLAYDES SMITH,
GEORGE BROWN, JAMES TAYLOR,
ROBERT MICKENS, EARL TOON,
DENNIS THOMAS, ROBERT BELL
and EUMIR DEODATO

Moderate R&B (♩ = 116)

NA NA HEY HEY KISS HIM GOODBYE

Words and Music by
GARY DE CARLO, DALE FRASHUER
and PAUL LEKA

32615

MY IMMORTAL

Words and Music by
BEN MOODY, AMY LEE
and DAVID HODGES

32615

NEW SOUL

Words and Music by
YAEL NAIM and DAVID DONATIEN

SMOOTH

Words and Music by
ITAAL SHUR and ROB THOMAS

OPEN ARMS

Words and Music by
JONATHAN CAIN and STEVE PERRY

(I CAN'T GET NO) SATISFACTION

Words and Music by
MICK JAGGER and **KEITH RICHARDS**

Moderately, driving (♩ = 132)

32615

OLD TIME ROCK & ROLL

Words and Music by
GEORGE JACKSON and
THOMAS E. JONES III

Moderate rock and roll (♩ = 126)

© 1977 (Renewed) MUSCLE SHOALS SOUND PUBLISHING CO., INC.
All Rights Reserved

TAKE IT EASY

Words and Music by
JACKSON BROWNE and GLENN FREY

STAIRWAY TO HEAVEN

Words and Music by
JIMMY PAGE and ROBERT PLANT

YOU AND ME

Words and Music by
JUDE COLE and JASON WADE

Moderately slow folk rock ($\quad$ = 138)
($\quad$ = 48 This represents the song pulse feel counted in one)

You and Me - 2 - 1
32615

Boulevard of Broken Dreams	Green Day
Celebration	Kool and the Gang
My Immortal	Evanescence
Na Na Hey Hey Kiss Him Goodbye	Steam
New Soul	Yael Naim
Old Time Rock & Roll	Bob Seger & The Silver Bullet Band
Open Arms	Journey
(I Can't Get No) Satisfaction	The Rolling Stones
Smooth	Santana featuring Rob Thomas
Stairway to Heaven	Led Zeppelin
Take It Easy	Eagles
You and Me	Lifehouse

This book is part of Alfred's *Easy Rock Instrumental Solos* series for Violin, Viola, and Cello. All string arrangements are fully compatible and can be successfully performed as ensembles or solos by students who have completed the first book of any standard string method. Each book features a removable string part, carefully arranged and edited with bowings, articulations, and keys well-suited to the Level 1 player, and includes piano accompaniments designed to be easily played by a teacher or intermediate piano student. A fully orchestrated accompaniment CD is also provided, featuring each song as a live performance demo track followed by a play-along track.

Books with matching songs are also part of Alfred's *Easy Rock Instrumental Solos* series for Flute, Clarinet, Alto Sax, Tenor Sax, Trumpet, Horn in F, and Trombone. All wind instrument books also include a fully orchestrated accompaniment CD, and an optional Piano Accompaniment book is available separately.

Due to level considerations regarding keys and instrument ranges, the wind instrument arrangements are not compatible with the string instrument arrangements in this series.

alfred.com

(I CAN'T GET NO) SATISFACTION

Words and Music by
MICK JAGGER and KEITH RICHARDS

(I Can't Get No) Satisfaction - 4 - 1
32615

(I Can't Get No) Satisfaction - 4 - 4
32615

OLD TIME ROCK & ROLL

Words and Music by
GEORGE JACKSON and
THOMAS E. JONES III

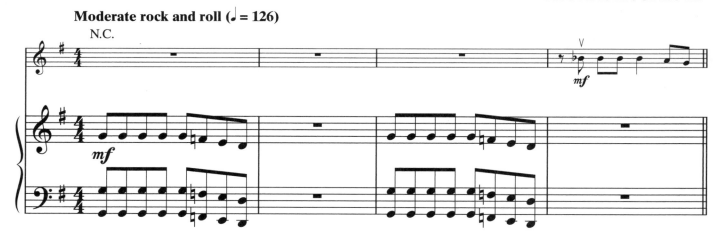

Old Time Rock & Roll - 3 - 1
32615

34

TAKE IT EASY

Words and Music by
JACKSON BROWNE and GLENN FREY

Take It Easy - 3 - 1
32615

STAIRWAY TO HEAVEN

Words and Music by
JIMMY PAGE and ROBERT PLANT

Moderately (♩ = 80)

(with pedal)

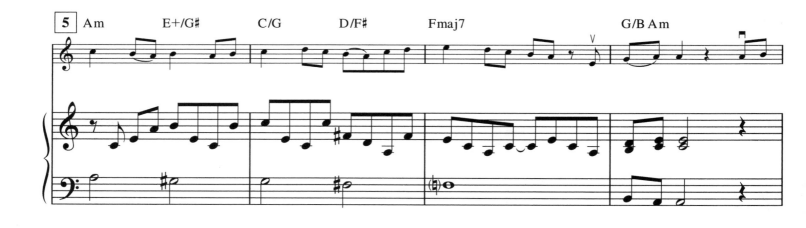

Stairway to Heaven - 4 - 1
32615

YOU AND ME

Words and Music by
JUDE COLE and JASON WADE

Moderately slow folk rock (♩ = 138)
(♩. = 48 This represents the song pulse feel counted in one)

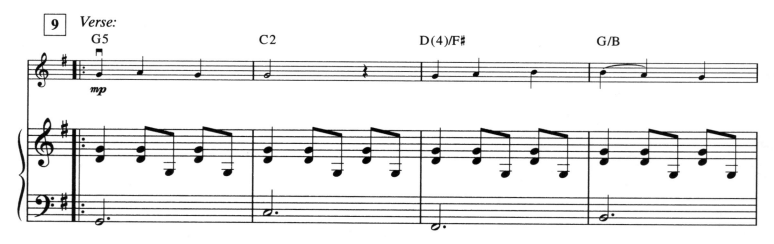

You and Me - 5 - 1
32615

You and Me - 5 - 2
32615

44